WEALDING THE WILLOW

A PORTRAIT OF ENGLISH VILLAGE GROUNDS
IN THE CRADLE OF CRICKET

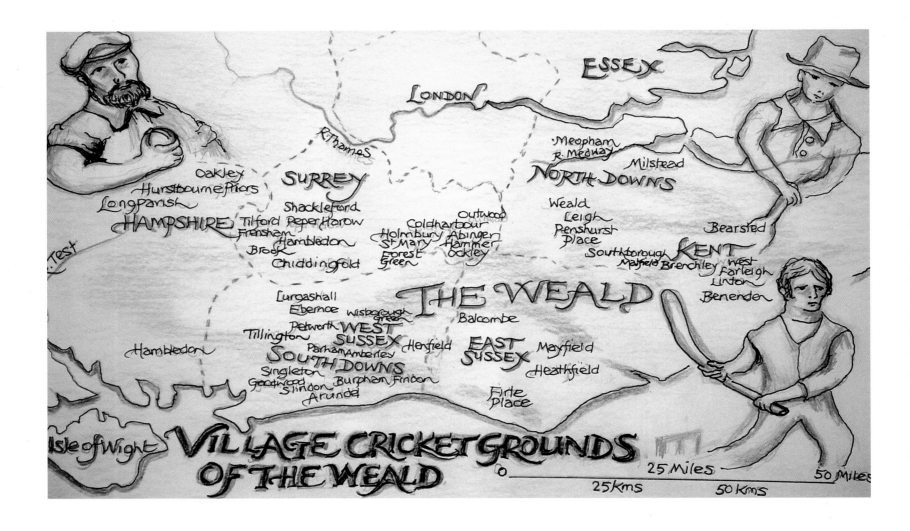

The map shows locations including:

ESSEX, **LONDON**

SURREY: Oakley, Hurstbourne Priors, Longparish, Shackleford, Tilford, Peper Harow, Frensham, Hambledon, Brook, Chiddingfold, Coldharbour, Holmbury St Mary, Abinger, Hammer, Forest Green, Ockley, Outwood

HAMPSHIRE

R. Test, R. Thames

NORTH DOWNS: Meopham, R. Medway, Milstead, Weald, Leigh, Penshurst Place, Southborough, Mayfield, Brenchley, Bearsted

KENT: West Farleigh, Linton, Benenden

THE WEALD

WEST SUSSEX: Lurgashall, Ebernoe, Petworth, Wisborough Green, Tillington, Parham, Amberley, Henfield, Balcombe, Hambledon

SOUTH DOWNS: Singleton, Goodwood, Slindon, Arundel, Burpham, Findon

EAST SUSSEX: Mayfield, Heathfield, Firle Place

Isle of Wight

VILLAGE CRICKET GROUNDS OF THE WEALD

0   25 Miles   50 Miles
25 Kms   50 Kms

In memory of my dear Mother and Father, who gave me the love of sport and cricket.

For Patch, Beans and Louise.

This book is also especially dedicated to Clare ('Clarers') for her endless support throughout my project and without whom the idea would never have seen the light of day. To my brother Ian, a 'proper writer', my sister Suzanne and Chris, who gave me the confidence to progress. To John Woodcock for all his immense help and finally to Richie Benaud for his encouragement and support for the book in writing his foreword for me.

ROBIN WHITCOMB

WEALDING THE WILLOW

A PORTRAIT OF ENGLISH VILLAGE GROUNDS IN THE CRADLE OF CRICKET

TEMPUS

ABOUT THE AUTHOR

Robin Whitcomb was born in Scarborough, Yorkshire in 1945. He was educated at Newlands School, Seaford and then at Cranleigh School in Surrey. After leaving school, Robin spent two years in America where in 1965 he joined up with Sonny and Cher as their drummer and played on their big hit 'I Got You Babe'. Returning to the UK, Robin played cricket for the MCC and rugby for Richmond RFC for ten years. He had an interesting two-year experience working for both the *Daily Telegraph* and the *Cricketer* magazine as E.W. Swanton's secretary. While at St Luke's College, Exeter he represented the South-West Counties *v.* South Africa and Fiji. He also played county rugby for Devon, Surrey and Buckinghamshire.

Robin lives in Wimbledon and teaches sport at Dulwich College Preparatory School in south-east London. He is an advanced cricket, rugby and tennis coach. Sport, photography and music have always been his main interests.

Robin has two sons, Patrick (20) and Giles (19), who are both in the music world.

First published 2005

Tempus Publishing Limited
The Mill, Brimscombe Port,
Stroud, Gloucestershire, GL5 2QG
www.tempus-publishing.com

British Library Cataloguing in Publication Data.
A catalogue record for this book is available from the British Library.

ISBN 0 7524 3457 8

Typesetting and origination by Tempus Publishing Limited.
Printed in Great Britain.

CONTENTS

ACKNOWLEDGEMENTS

Sincere thanks to all the people who were kind enough to help me start *Wealding the Willow*.

START OF PLAY

Monica Jensen, Valley of the Rocks, Devon; Nick Constable, Lynton & Lynmouth CC; Abigail Deacon, Bridgeman Art Gallery; Roger Chown, originally at the Club Cricket Conference; Stephen Green, formerly of the MCC Library, Lord's Cricket Ground, Richard 'Wittsy' Witts, my original Kent 'sherpa'; Sally ('Sallybags') Lewis for her help and fun both in Sussex and Surrey; Alan Perkins for Sussex village details and Mike Donnelly and John Collins for Kent.

THE MIDDLE ORDER

KENT
Meopham: Barbara Wade. Milstead: Roger Chapman.
Southborough: Andrew Hinds. Bearsted: Rosemary Pearce and Ian Lambert.
Benenden: Peter Blockley. Penshurst: Richard Banks and Simon Leegood.
West Farleigh: Ian Payne. Linton Park: John Thirkell.
Brenchley: Alan Jones. Matfield: Simon Knott, Weald: Dave Stringer.

SUSSEX
Singleton: John Baker and Martin Davies. Lurgashall: Rory Lawson.
Goodwood: Richard Geffin. Slindon: Graham Ball.
Arundel: Tina Hawkins and 'Chitty'. Petworth: 'Jumbo' Taylor.
Amberley: Keith Dalmon and Paul Challon.
Findon: Frank Higgens, Nick and Josh Gifford. Balcombe: Albert Constable.
Heathfield: Hazel Ticehurst. Mayfield: Paul McColl.
Wisborough Green: Ken Vickery. Firle Place: Roger Steadman.
Parham: Brian Huffer. Ebernoe: Richard Stemp. Tillington: Graham Pooley.
Burpham: Tim Caffyn.

SURREY
Hambledon: Mary Parker and Arthur Blackman.
Coldharbour: Terry Knight. Brook: Brian Devonport and Helen Haslam.
Tilford: Clive Thursby. Ockley: Loll Figg.
Abinger Hammer: Geoff and Sue Dunn. Outwood: Adrian Christie.
Chiddingfold: Simon Thorpe. Shackleford: Nick Swan.
Forest Green: Tim Ives. Frensham: Alan and Pat Stone.
Peper Harow: Michael Tait.

HAMPSHIRE
Longparish: Allen Snow, John Woodcock and Geoff Hayes.
Hambledon: John Shakeshaft and John Carroll.
Oakley: Sally Warner.
Hurstbourne Priors: Geoff and Sally Rampton and Martyn Page.

TOWARDS THE END OF THE INNINGS

My sincere thanks to all the many friends who helped me in the final stages of the book. Holly Bennion, Rob Sharman and James Howarth from Tempus Publishing who gave me so much help and advice.

At Dulwich College Prep School: Matthew Woodard, Katy Fletcher for all her enormous encouragement throughout the course of this book and preventing my overuse of adjectives; to David, Martin, Ann, Paul, Nick and Matthew in the IT department for bailing me out on numerous occasions.

At Kingston: Carol at Jessops Photography. At Roehampton: Peter Beim for his assistance with the layout and to Ian and Val Lanceley for all their support. At Wimbledon: Manish Patel, the technical wizard, who spent hours sorting out hundreds of picture images and text.

FOREWORD

BY RICHIE BENAUD

No harm is done to cricket devotees if occasionally we are reminded there is a world outside Test and other international cricket; that the game exists, and in fact knows few boundaries, even in the whizz-bang lifestyle of the modern times.

I have always been of the opinion that cricket in any era has reflected life itself. That can be seen today as it could equally have been seen more than 250 years ago when the first code of rules evolved. In *Wealding the Willow* Robin Whitcomb has captured with delightful photographs and explanatory text the early days of the game where it all began in the Weald area of South East England.

Because of my personal experience of having played at Longparish and Wisborough Green, their pages caught my eye. At the former ground I clashed with what one might term a 'proper' blacksmith, one who had come that morning straight from the forge to the ground and proceeded to uphold the reputation of all blacksmith-cricketers. It was a new experience for me to bowl to him and for the umpires instantly to have to call for another ball, so far had the wrong'un I had produced been struck into the distance.

Slindon is another delightful village with a splendid ground. Their players were once good enough to defeat the All England team. It is said that when the aristocracy, and for that matter the gamblers, decided cricket was the game for them, matches would be played for 1,000 guineas a side. Translated into modern money they were jousting for £70,000 and, apart from those major bets, there would be plenty of other wagers going on around the ground as well. Not all of them were decided in calm fashion!

The game has evolved in extraordinary fashion over centuries and, according to Richard Daft, there was a time when the bowler was allowed to make the pitch to suit himself. There are a few modern-day bowlers who would be delighted if the same rules applied these days.

Bowling has evolved from under-arm, to round-arm, or, as it was also known, 'high-handed', to over-arm, and Christine Willes, the sister of Kent bowler John Willes, is the lady who can take the credit for that. Her voluminous hooped skirts precluded an under-arm delivery, so she simply raised her arm. We are all indebted to her.

In *Wealding the Willow* there are many delightful touches concerning the game of cricket as it was at the beginning and in the early days as it grew into the great sport it is today. It strikes a chord with me because I have never lost my love of the written word, despite having been part of other areas of the media. It is an appreciation generated by the fact that my father was a school teacher who loved books and the English language.

Robin Whitcomb has done us and cricket proud with this book and I hope you enjoy it as much as I have.

Richie Benaud

INTRODUCTION

How many times have cricket lovers like myself driven slowly by a village cricket ground and been tempted to pull in and watch just one or two or even three deliveries by the bowler?

There are so many little village cricket grounds I never knew existed. By chance I came across the Lynton & Lynmouth ground in the Valley of the Rocks, Devon. The sight was so spectacular that it prompted me to try and put a book together about village cricket grounds so that devotees of the game will have the opportunity to share my experience. I have based my book on the Weald because it was where the game first started and has been known as 'The Cradle of Cricket'.

There are many attractive village grounds I have sadly missed out in this book. I hope that I will have the opportunity to include these if possible in a future book, so do please contact me with your recommendations:

robinwhitcomb@ukonline.co.uk

Opposite page: 'Tossing for Innings' by Robert James, *c.* 1841

THE EARLY DAYS OF CRICKET

No one really knows how cricket first began. There was not a magical moment similar to when William Webb Ellis supposedly picked up the ball at Rugby School and with a 'total disregard of the rules of the game' ran on to score. What is known is that it took centuries for cricket to evolve and develop into the game we know today.

There are references to cricket in the early seventeenth century but these were mostly concerned with violent incidents in the crude version then played. Few matches went on without fights breaking out among the spectators – and even the players too. There was a great deal at stake from betting on the final outcome or on individual players. One of the earliest mentions of the game was of Thomas Wilson, a person of a 'certain Puritan divine' being suspended by the Archbishop Laud for playing cricket on the Lord's Day in 1640 in Maidstone, Kent. Nine more parishioners, again from Kent, were banned fifteen years later and fined the considerable amount of two shillings for playing on the Lord's Day. The 'gospel' very soon spread as far away as Aleppo, Syria, where on 6 May 1676, a naval chaplain, Henry Teonge, recorded how he and a party from three of His Majesty's ships 'did in a fine valley pitch a princely tent and divert themselves with various sports including "Krickett"'.

The shape of the game in the early days was very basic. In *A History of Cricket* the eminent cricket historian H.S. Altham refers to a pastime of 'club-ball', the generic ancestor of most of the English ball games. The primitive bat and ball game began in the Weald area, which incorporated the western part of Kent and into Sussex between the North and South Downs. The game started here due to the large forests in the Weald. Trees were felled for the construction of shipbuilding and making houses. In between working hours, the labourers would enjoy the pursuit of this 'club-ball' with a bat made up from handy wooden remnants. This early pastime then established itself into other parts of the Weald extending out to Surrey and Hampshire.

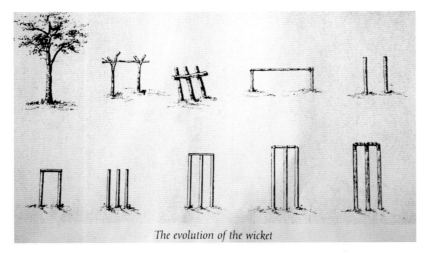

The evolution of the wicket

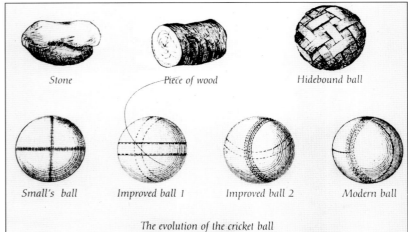

Stone   *Piece of wood*   *Hidebound ball*

Small's ball   *Improved ball 1*   *Improved ball 2*   *Modern ball*

The evolution of the cricket ball

Village cricket in the Weald attracted all sorts of people of different social standing. Wealthy landowners of vast estates selected their cricket teams from their tenants and servants. The remainder of the side could contain the local vicar or tradesmen. This made for a healthy social mix but the division between the aristocracy and the servants was often conspicuous. Lamborn, a farmer and the first recognized off-spinner, was regarded as 'a plain-spoken little bumpkin'. Once, when bowling to the Duke of Dorset, he narrowly missed the Duke's leg stump and in his broad Hampshire dialect, Lamborn's excitement had to be contained as he said to the Duke: 'Ah, it was tedious near you, sir'.

As the attraction of cricket spread amongst the great landowners (see Goodwood Park, Firle Place, Linton Park and Penshurst Place), competition was strong between the various estates with each landlord desperately trying to select the most powerful team. Lumpy Stevens, an extremely accurate bowler, lived on Tankerville's estate. Minshull, probably the foremost batsman in the 'England' sides who played against Hambledon, was a gardener to the Duke of Dorset. At Linton Park, Tom Peach was an outstanding bowler who was employed as head groundsman and huntsman with the Linton Beagles.

'Gamesters' was the name given to the players representing the landowner's team. The payment for their appearance came from the patron who organised the match and he would hope to recoup his expenses from the raising of stakes or wagers on the game. Sums of 500 to 1,000 guineas were quite common stakes on matches, which were often watched by as many as 20,000 spectators who could place bets themselves either on the team or on an individual's performance.

Cricket differs from other games inasmuch as it has laws and not rules. These laws assume unquestioned support by players. In days long past and even today to a lesser degree, the basic legalities became restrictive. The first set of laws called 'Articles of Agreement' were drawn up in 1727 by the 2nd Duke of Richmond of Goodwood and Mr Brodrick of Peper Harow, near Godalming. The eleventh article of agreement read: 'That there shall be one Umpire of each side; & that if any of the Gamesters shall speak or give their opinion, on any point of the Game, they are to be turned out & voided in the Match; this not to extend to the Duke of Richmond and Mr Brodrick.' The first official laws of the game were formed in 1744 with revisions in 1755, 1774 and 1786. In 1887 it was illegal to declare an innings closed before all the wickets had been taken. John Shuter, the captain of Surrey, ordered four of his batsmen to get themselves out by hitting their own wickets or standing outside the crease so as to get themselves

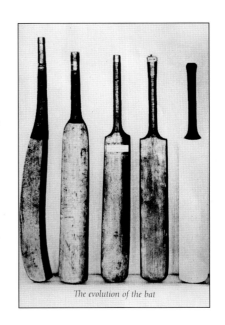

The evolution of the bat

stumped. After 1835 a team failing to reach a certain number of runs short of their opponents' first innings total were required to follow on, whether the other team liked it or not. This would mean that the team batting last had to put up with a well-worn pitch after fielding twice in succession. Playing for Essex in 1897, F.G. Bull showed initiative in preventing opponents Lancashire falling short of his team's total. He simply bowled wides to the boundary. The leg-before law came in in 1888, and was a rare form of dismissal: it was not the done thing to use pads rather than the bat. One of the most extraordinary laws of the original set of 1744 was the change from the accepted ruling that a batsman could take a swipe at a fielder with his bat when he was about to be caught out. In 1624 a young fielder named Jasper Vinall, when fielding, was reportedly killed in this way. The laws were then altered so that the batsman was only permitted to shoulder-barge the fielder as he went to make the catch.

One of the most noticeable changes in the development of cricket was the style of bowling. In the early days underarm bowling was used to great effect. At the Artillery Ground in London a match was played between five of the Hambledon Club and five of All England. John Small, an early bat-and-ball maker, was the last Hambledon player in and only needed fourteen runs to win. He managed this but only after Lumpy Stevens had bowled the ball three times between the two stumps (measuring one foot high and two feet across) without disturbing the crosspiece or bail. As a result the Hambledon Club introduced the third stump and the two bails were in circulation by 1786. The bowling action was then experimented on, with the introduction of a round-arm style – possibly introduced when ladies began playing cricket and found that their skirts hindered their underarm bowling. Alfred Mynn, the 'Lion of Kent' bowled very fast with a round-arm action but in 1816 a law was passed preventing this action being used. There was a period of uncertainty concerning the laws of bowling and in 1822 John Willes used his new straight-arm bowling action when playing for Kent against the MCC at Lord's. The umpire, Noah Mann (a godson of one of the most powerful patrons of the game, Sir Horace Mann) continuously no-balled the bowler. In his anger, Willes threw the ball down and 'jumped on his horse, and rode away out of Lord's and out of cricket history'. Yet straight-arm bowling was continued in matches and an outstanding exponent of this style was William Lillywhite from Sussex. It wasn't until 1835 that over-arm or straight-arm bowling was made legitimate.

Laws about the regulation size of the bat arrived in 1771 when Thomas 'Shock' White wielded a bat as wide as the stumps (two feet) in the match Surrey & Kent v. Middlesex & Hampshire. He scored 197 and as a result a law was made that the width of the bat in future must be four-and-a-quarter inches.

Much of the development of the game had its origins at the Hambledon Club in Hampshire. Since its formation around 1750 the club had a marked influence on the game and had attracted the very best cricketers in the Weald. The strange fact is that Hambledon village was miles from anywhere and so half the county would pitch upon Hambledon when they played distinguished sides such as an 'All-England' team or the Slindon club from neighbouring Sussex. There were notable Hambledon professional players such as John Nyren and his father Richard, who ran the Bat & Ball Inn across the road from the Broadhalfpenny ground. Richard was both captain and secretary of Hambledon for many years. Spectators in their thousands would turn up, many on horseback, to watch the very best cricketers in the land. For three decades Hambledon attracted both the cream of professional players and the chief patrons of cricket.

The evolution of Cricket dress

Top: 'Lumpy Stevens'
Below: Richard Nyren

These were the halcyon days of Hambledon when cricket had reached a new level of performance and the famous Hambledon players led the way. This was the period of change and inventiveness – a time when batsmen crafted their skills to defend against the length delivery with a straight bat. But by 1787 Hambledon was in decline. Club meetings were not well supported, which was particularly sad for the Reverend Charles Powlett who had spent thirty years of his life assembling the greatest players together into one club. An entry from one of the last meetings at Hambledon read: 'a wet day, only three members present, nine bottles of wine'. By 1796 the shutters were down. The following year Richard Nyren, who had been the mainstay of this great club, died, with Hambledon so close to his heart. Most of the same Patrons, Sir Horace Mann, The Duke of Dorset and other prominent cricketing dignitaries, decided that the game had moved on, and that London and Lord's would be the headquarters and the future of cricket in England. The curved-bat-and-ball game with a 'wicket' gate was now a relic of the past. Cricket pressed on to the next important chapter of its history. The game had established itself as a national pastime and one that had crossed all social boundaries.

THE START OF CRICKET IN THE WEALD

Although it is difficult to trace the origins of cricket – due to the total lack of written sources – it is much easier to understand the reason why the game began to be played extensively in the Weald area of South East England. Originally the land between the Downs and the south coast was one continuous tract of forest. By the seventeenth century a good deal of it had been cleared. The trees had been felled mainly to provide materials for the building of houses and ships. During their leisure breaks from work, the forestry labourers enjoyed playing a bat and ball game. The bat was cut to shape from the plentiful supplies of wood and the ball was carved and shaped as round as possible to be held in the hand. The underarm bowler aimed to hit the tree stump behind the batsman.

Although cricket developed in the woodlands of the Weald, it was also played on the open chalk downlands. This allowed the game to take place in plenty of space and the springy turf was ideal to run on and provide a very playable surface. The other great advantage was that, with such a multitude of sheep grazing on the downlands, the turf became closely cropped and this provided ideal playing conditions for bat and ball games. In these downlands of Sussex the shepherds introduced bowling to hit a 'wicket gate' through which the flocks of sheep would pass. The upright sticks became known as stumps (derived from the original tree stump target) and lying flat across one stick to the other was a crosspiece that became known as a bail.

The game of cricket developed in the Weald. There is evidence of early seventeenth century matches taking place throughout Kent, Surrey, Sussex and Hampshire – the area known as the Weald, 'The Cradle of Cricket'.

KENT

BEARSTED

The year 1750 is generally accepted as the foundation of the Hambledon Club and its importance in cricketing history cannot be underestimated, although only a short time before this the Whitehall Evening Post (of 15 August 1749) reported on a match between The Gentlemen of Bearsted and The Gentlemen of London. The term 'The Cradle of Cricket' did not only refer to Hambledon but also to the Weald of Kent where Bearsted is considered to be one of the great nurseries of the noble game.

Bearsted Green was positively confirmed as a cricketing venue with a reference in the *Kentish Evening Post* to Bearsted playing Hadlow on 25 July 1750. At this time Robert Clifford emerged as a truly great player. He was an all-rounder who played for Kent and England. While the famous cricketer Richard Nyren was running the Bat & Ball Inn at Hambledon, Clifford kept the White Horse Inn next to the green at Bearsted.

During the period 1800-1849 there were strong links with the village of Leeds. Indeed, some of the matches were played as a combined 'Bearsted & Leeds XI'. This was the time when the great England cricketer Alfred Mynn played for Bearsted. Mynn was a large man, 6ft 1in tall and weighing over eighteen stone. He was a legendary folk-hero of Kentish cricket and was known as 'The Lion of Kent'. The comparison of Alfred Mynn to

W.G. Grace is apt, for each in his age was a national institution. Mynn died in 1861 and he is buried under the shade of a yew tree in a corner of Thurnham churchyard. So popular was he as a Kentish champion that 400 of his large circle of admiring friends united together to afford and erect Mynn's tombstone.

Another famous Bearsted personality was Baroness Orczy, the author of The Scarlet Pimpernel. The hero in the book, Sir Percy Blakeney, was not dissimilar in aristocratic affectation to the author. When her carriage drawn by horses approached her house, Snowfield, a horn was sounded and the domestic staff had to assemble in two lines standing to attention in the hall. They then bowed as the Baroness entered the house.

BENENDEN

Cricket has been played in Benenden since the late eighteenth century. The first recorded match on the green was in August 1798 against a team from Wittersham. The great days of the village side were from 1825 to 1838 when such stalwarts as Edward Wenman and Richard Mills played for both Benenden and Kent.

Betting in cricket was prolific at this time. A wager was offered in 1830 by the 'nine natives of the Parish of Benenden with two given men (who) will play with any Eleven Gentlemen of the County of Kent for £20 to £100 a side'.

In more recent years Benenden Green has been the scene of many celebrity matches. In 1984 Alan Ealham and Derek Underwood took on a Benenden team to celebrate the 150th anniversary of a match first played in 1834.

BRENCHLEY

Brenchley Cricket Club is conveniently situated in the village and it is a gloriously peaceful setting, perched up high with the church in the background. The first recorded game was in 1749 when a Brenchley Parish team played Ham Street. This was supposedly one of the earliest games played in Kent. In one corner of the cricket field are two great oak trees and below there is a wooded valley.

The ground also has a claim to fame as Siegfried Sassoon (1886-1967), the famous First World War poet and writer, was known to have played cricket at Brenchley. Sassoon wrote a collection of poems on cricket and he even wrote about a game at Brenchley itself in a book entitled *The Flower Show Match*. He changed the names of those who actually played in the book, although he did mention the two old oak trees on the outfield. In 1986 the club had a 'Siegfried Sassoon Centenary Match' against the Imperial War Museum. This conjures up a warlike picture of a plethora of 'sledging' and even a return to the seventeenth-century cricket ruling where a batsman could physically obstruct a fielder trying to catch him out.

The village is noted for its fine Tudor cottages and even the butcher's shop is timber-framed. Brenchley enjoy playing friendly cricket on Sundays. Members and friends of the Sports & Social Club can enjoy a picnic, catch up with village gossip and occasionally watch the cricket.

LINTON PARK

L inton has a long tradition of being a family ground. For over two centuries fathers, sons and brothers have played cricket on this classic hilltop ground in a secluded woodland setting.

The club was founded in 1787 by Sir Horace Mann. Grand county matches were played here with Sir Horace backing Kent for sums between 100 and 500 guineas. Sadly, with his fortune spent, Sir Horace was forced to leave Linton. In 1815 the estate was passed on by marriage to the Cornwallis family. In 1883 Mr Fiennes Cornwallis inherited the title and the first project he carried out was to improve the ground. The cricket square was renewed and the pavilion was built. Still standing today, it is an excellent example of ornate Victorian cast-ironwork. An unusual sight is the hawthorn bush just inside the midwicket boundary – often well guarded by a fielder trying to save four runs.

Another legendary figure in the history of the club is Tom Peach. In 1885 he became the head groundsman and huntsman with the Linton Beagles. The latter kept Tom fit for he was often required to bowl for most of the day! For years Tom Peach was synonymous with Linton Park. His descendants, the Thirkell family, are the mainstay of Linton Park to this day.

LEIGH

Cricket has been played at Leigh for over 300 years. In the early 1700s matches on Fair Days attracted large crowds on the green. As well as the cricket, there were many side-shows, betting stalls and food and ale tents.

Betting was prevalent throughout the Weald. By the 1740s cricket was attracting the attention of moralists, who believed that the lower orders ought to be at work instead of idly watching or betting on results. Although cricket was originally believed to be a peasant sport, it had become a fascination for the aristocracy and the gentry. Gambling on either individual players or on the result was endemic throughout the 1800s. Upwards of £1,000 was often seen changing hands.

Leigh Cricket Club reached its peak in the late eighteenth century. The most outstanding bowler was William Burchard, who played for Kent and England. Timothy Duke, a member of the famous Duke & Son cricket ball-making family, also represented the county and England too. In those days, the leather Duke ball was bowled underarm (often with fast 'sneaks') to hit a wicket two feet apart and one foot high.

Leigh is situated just to the west of Tonbridge and it is one of many appealing Wealden villages in the area. It has a green of seven acres, which qualifies it to be one of Kent's largest. Meanwhile, the village church looks down upon the cricket pitch while the obligatory local pub is in easy reach after the game. Today you can visit the green at Leigh on any weekend and see the club flag flying from the pavilion flagpole, proudly displaying the date 1700. There is plenty of cricket for both young and old with the many juniors practising in the mornings and the loyal lady supporters taking tea from their hampers in the late afternoon.

MATFIELD

The origins of Matfield Green Cricket Club are uncertain; however, it is a relatively new club compared to the other villages in Kent. It was founded in the early 1970s, where the game flourished through to the 1980s. Mr Jack Wish was one of the founder members and it was through his dedication to the club that the pavilion was developed. Another former player, Mr Charlie Sales, remains an avid supporter, although he remarks that 'it was a different game in my day, son'. Matfield ran a strong and successful side in village league cricket but sadly in 1990 the club temporarily lost its way. Happily cricket was soon resurrected by loyal members such as Mr Simon Knott.

In 2001, Derek Underwood of Kent and England, who was living in the village at the time, played a game on the green for Matfield and it was a pleasure for the club when he re-opened the newly refurbished pavilion. Mostly friendly matches were played on the green and in seasons 2002 and 2003 Matfield entered the National Village Competition.

Matfield village green is one of many idyllic cricket settings in Kent. The green itself is one of the largest in the county. It is surrounded by many attractive old and new houses, some of which are fine tile-hung buildings so typical of Kent. There is also a striking Georgian house dating back to 1728. Many Wealden villages that once had 'greens' now have little squares and the green at Matfield is so large that it could be termed as a common. In fact, the Anglo-Saxon name for a large clearing is 'feld' and the village name comes from the word 'Matta'.

Another appealing aspect of Matfield is the duck pond at the far end of the green. It is a useful attraction for mum and the children to quietly escape from dad on the cricket field. Just behind the duck pond is the Star Inn – very conveniently positioned for the cricketers. Like many villages, the third part of village life involves the church. St Luke's has an unusual timbered section and spire perched aloft the main roof.

MEOPHAM

There are few players who would deny that Meopham Green is a unique place to play cricket. The main road is so close to the boundary that one false step by a fielder chasing the ball and he could be confronted by a double-decker bus. Meopham cricket club is steeped in history. There are references to the club as far back as 1773. This was the same year that the first known bat makers, Pett of Sevenoaks, were making straight bats and charging four shillings and sixpence for their best blades.

One of Kent's prettiest cricket greens is at Meopham – pronounced 'Meppam'. The green is surrounded by attractive cottages and a windmill. The fully restored black smock mill dates back to 1821.

Meopham produced some outstanding cricketers during its history. Perhaps the most legendary was Valentine Romney, who captained Kent in the famous match against All-England in 1744.

Over deep midwicket and just across the busy road is The Cricketers Inn, which dates back to 1735. It is thought to be the oldest hostelry so-named in England. The great matches of the 1830s were often spread over two days and visiting teams would be well and truly entertained in the evening at The Cricketers. There were often many sore heads in the field the next day and certainly some much-needed sleep on the return journey by horse and carriage.

MILSTEAD

Milstead Cricket Club was founded in 1857. The rustic-looking timbered pavilion with its thatched roof was started in 1948 with carpenters from Sheerness Dockyard. The club was originally known as the Frinsted & Milstead Cricket Club. In the beginning it was the influential local vicar who set out a strict code of rules. He insisted that all meetings would be held in the local school classroom and not in the pub: 'The public house is ill befitting for the purpose of meetings as it could lead to immorality and destroy innocent recreation.'

The early years were a struggle to find a team. For away matches Milsted (as it was then known) sometimes travelled in a conveyance, paying the driver 14 shillings to take them. The alliance with Frinsted was eventually terminated in 1877 and by the 1900s the club was playing regularly again. Funds were raised from whist drives and dances in the village hall. They event went as far as fining a fielder one penny for dropping a catch and three pennies if the batsman made a duck. Today Milstead is one of the best established clubs in the Sittingbourne district. Just to the right of the pavilion is a little scorebox in matching reed-thatch.

PENSHURST PLACE

Penshurst Place Cricket Club was founded in 1752. It is the oldest privately owned cricket club in England and it was started at a time when interest in cricket was increasing among the nobility. Even earlier, in 1728, the park at Penshurst was the venue for a cricket match between William Gage's Sussex team and a Kent team led by Edwin Stead. 'The Kent men have been too expert for those of Sussex,' remarked Stead. So, with a winner's purse of 50 guineas, Kent became the first county champions on the famous Penshurst Place ground.

Penshurst Place, the finest fourteenth-century manor house in England, is owned and managed by Viscount De L'Isle (a descendant of Sir Philip Sidney, Elizabethan poet and soldier), whose family have resided there for generations. There is the magnificent Barons Hall and a marvellous collection of paintings, furniture, tapestries and armour. The gardens surrounding the house are of Elizabethan design dating back to 1346. Penshurst Place is so famous that people often forget there is also an attractive village there.

The cricket club is unique in that it has played on the same site since its foundation. Cricketers from around the world have relished the experience of playing on this beautifully manicured ground and the magnificent view of the house and its surrounds.

PENSHURST PARK
CRICKET CLUB
This is the oldest privately
owned cricket ground in the world.
It is thought that the first
cricket match took place in 1723/24
President:-
VISCOUNT DE L'ISLE M.B.E.

SOUTHBOROUGH

This advertisement celebrates the earliest match on Southborough Common. In those days the captain who won the toss of the coin would decide on where he would like the pitch to be placed. 'A good ordinary' was the set lunch on the day.

One of the most famous cricketers from Southborough was John Willes. He was responsible for the reintroduction of round-arm bowling. Unfortunately, while playing for Kent *v*. MCC at Lord's in 1822, he was immediately no-balled due to his radical bowling action. In a fit of rage Willes threw down the ball in disgust, jumped on his horse and rode furiously out of the hallowed ground. Frank Woolley, a great left-hand batsmen for Kent and England from 1909, lived in Southborough and often attended many social functions at the club.

The Maidstone Journal & Kentish Advertiser
Tuesday 22 July 1794

A Match of Cricket will be played at Southborough on Friday next between the gentlemen of Tonbridge and the gentlemen of Chiddingstone, Penshurst and Leigh. The wickets to be pitched at ten o'clock and the game to be played out. A good ordinary is arranged for two o'clock at the Hand & Sceptre.

WEST FARLEIGH

The cricket club at West Farleigh is relatively young compared to many neighbouring grounds in the Weald. In fact the football club began first in 1911 and then a cricket club was founded in 1920. These clubs amalgamated in 1927 to form the West Farleigh Sports Club. Along with the church, the sports club provides the major source of events in the village today.

At the beginning of the nineteenth century West Farleigh was a bustling community of 390 inhabitants. It was renowned for its hops and fruit orchards and village life centred not only around farming but also the parish church of All Saints, which dates back to 1589. Today the village population is little changed but the hops and fruit trees are long gone. Reminders of those early days are few but the three pubs are still in existence and the parish church is a thriving haven for the many social functions.

WEALD

The first recorded game played at the Weald Club was in 1895. The match was against local rivals Ide Hill and this fixture is still closely contested today. Originally cricket matches were played on the village green but now the club play on a very attractive ground just south of the village. The Wealden setting is so distinctive and the pavilion is Grade Two listed. On a Saturday afternoon there is the cricket match in the foreground and the farmer working hard on his tractor in the background.

SUSSEX

AMBERLEY

Amberley Cricket Club formed around 1870. The club has always played on the parish ground with views stretching out towards the South Downs. Like many village cricket clubs a peppercorn rent is paid for the ground each year. The club played friendly matches until the mid-1980s and then joined a local league. When this league folded, the club returned to friendly matches once more. In 1998 the attraction to return to more competitive cricket was such that the club joined the West Sussex League. Amberley has enjoyed much success over the past few years. Although league cricket is more intense, the club still retains a sense of fun and enjoyment and often, after the game, the players will retire to the local pub, nicknamed the Pink Pony. It is, in fact, the Black Horse.

Amberley village is spread out over a low ridge overlooking 30 square miles of grazing marshes watered by the river Arun. The village is an ancient place whose name means 'fields yellow with buttercups'. Originally, in AD 680, lands in this area were granted to St Wilfred, the missionary who converted the South Saxons to Christianity. The Norman church was rebuilt in the twelfth century. Amberley Castle was built in 1380 as a fortified summer palace for the Bishops of Chichester. It is more of a manor house than a castle (today it is a privately owned luxury hotel) and it is believed that Charles II took refuge there during his flight to France in 1651. At the same time, it is also alleged that Charles II stopped for refreshments at the nearby George & Dragon Inn at Houghton.

ARUNDEL

The cricket club at Arundel is just a short distance away from the castle. The game was first played there in 1702. Sadly, however, the history of the club has been lost in the mists of time, although what is known is that a match was played between the Men of Arundel and an East Sussex XI in 1771. Certainly cricket has been played at the present ground at Waterwoods Plain for a long time. The original thatched pavilion was built in 1884 and a celebration match was played to mark its centenary.

Arundel was a settlement before the Romans invaded. It was one of William the Conqueror's most favoured knights, Roger de Montgomery, who first built a castle here on the high ground overlooking the river in the late eleventh century. It is the second-largest castle in England and it has been the seat of the Dukes of Norfolk and the Earls of Arundel for over 700 years. Inside the castle there can be seen some fine furniture dating from the sixteenth century and there are some excellent tapestries and paintings

by Reynolds, Van Dyck, Gainsborough, Holbein and Constable. The Duke of Norfolk's elegant cricket ground lies just outside the castle and overseas international teams often play here at the start of their tours.

Like most cricket clubs Arundel played only friendly games in the very early days. But, in order to exist and attract players, Arundel joined both the Sussex Invitation League and the West Sussex League. Extensive changes (particularly to the pavilion) have taken place at the club in the recent past and today Arundel, with a busy cricket fixture list, has managed to retain its friendly atmosphere.

BALCOMBE

Balcombe Cricket Club is tucked away down a winding lane. The ground stands high up with views over the Sussex countryside. It is comfortably distanced from the noisy traffic of the A23. The ground is quite unique, as the playing area or 'square' is high up on a brow. A fielder deep on one side of the ground is unable to see his teammate fielding deep on the opposite side.

One of the earliest records is of the unusual game played at Balcombe against Ifield in 1869. MCC records report 'the match being one of the very few instances where the opposing teams scored exactly the same number of runs in each innings, 44 and 24 respectively'.

Just up from the cricket field is the village of Balcombe with its attractive eighteenth-century cottages. Balcombe railway station is on the main London to Brighton line and in days gone by this was very convenient for players to travel by train to Balcombe for cricket matches.

BURPHAM & WARNINGCAMP

The club was formed in 1880 by Mr E. Dawtrey Drewitt, the Squire of Burpham village, who lived in Peppering House. Adjoining the house was a field and, being a cricket lover, he landscaped his own cricket ground. There are magnificent views over the river Arun with the castle as a majestic backcloth. Drewitt invited cricketing friends, among whom were Dr W.G. Grace and Ranjitsinjhi, to play for his Burpham team against visiting sides.

During a match against an Oxford University college team, a Drewitt cousin asked a pale young player what he would do after leaving Oxford and he replied, 'I'll go back to Africa.' Later she asked the college captain the name of the player and he replied, 'Oh! That's Cecil Rhodes.' The painter John Ruskin also played on the Peppering ground and he described the view as 'the second most beautiful in Europe.' He did not say which he considered to be the most beautiful – perhaps it was a view in Italy where he had lived, or in the Lake District where he was living at the time he made this remark.

At the turn of the century, after Mr Drewitt passed away, his successor required the field for farming purposes. The cricket club relocated from place to place and eventually, in 1931, the club moved to its present attractive ground with the support and encouragement of the 16th Duke of Norfolk.

The ground is on Burpham Camp, which is a National Monument, being one of Alfred the Great's Saxon strongholds in the tenth century against the marauding Danes. King Alfred built five forts between Lewes and Chichester and 'Burgham', its original name, was in the middle of these. The club emblem has the head of a Saxon chief.

After the Second World War the club combined with the nearby village of Warningcamp. It is believed that this name came from the advantageous position of the Saxon rampart, from where they could see the Danes advancing from the coast and could duly signal a warning to the defending Saxon camps. Burpham's remarkable history also includes records of a leper colony that was in the Sussex village of Findon. The trail between the two villages is called 'Leper's Path'. They would walk in columns over the downs ringing a bell so as to warn anybody around of their presence. No other church in the Diocese would receive the lepers except St Mary's, Burpham. Today there is a uniqueness about life in this very pretty downland village and the cricket legacy of Mr E. Dawtrey Drewitt has continued at Burpham.

EBERNOE

Ebernoe is tucked away in the north-west corner of Sussex. It is a scattered hamlet near Petworth, with only 200 inhabitants and a distance of 42 miles from London. It is remote enough even today to evade the tourists and a mention in the guidebooks. It can, however, claim at least one reference in *The Times*, where, on 11 April 1938, it was reported that 'summer time is not recognized by the 200 inhabitants of Ebernoe... they sleep on for another hour.'

Ebernoe comes to life once a year on 25 July, St James's Day, when the Horn Fair takes place. The fair is at least 500 years old. It was revived in its present form by the Victorians, who introduced cricket to the occasion. The revival possibly came from the influence of the Sheep Fair at Findon in Sussex. The Horn Fair celebrations begin with a cricket match on the attractive little ground surrounded by woods on the Leconfield Estate. A road bisects the outfield of the ground and the fielders often have to scamper across this at their peril when chasing a ball. Sometimes a car travelling by can suddenly alter the direction of the retrieving fielder. While the cricket is being played, a horned sheep is put to roast in a pit just outside the boundary line of the ground. Spectators not only watch the cricket but also observe those experienced in the difficult art of spit roasting and basting the sheep in oil. All being well the meat will be ready by lunchtime and the cricketers and their opponents (normally the neighbouring Lurgashall team) will, like their predecessors, feast off the sheep at the end of the morning's play.

The cricket match is always full of fun with some mighty hitting and very often some close-run games. At the end of play – usually at about six o'clock in the evening – comes the high point of the celebrations: the presentation of the head and the horns of the sheep to the player who has scored the most runs on the winning side. Horns are an old symbol of the cuckold or deceived husband that goes back to medieval times. The bawdy licentious behaviour of long, long ago is in strong contrast to the gentle playing of cricket and the sedate ceremony of today.

FINDON

The first mention of there being a cricket club in the village can be found in the *West Sussex Gazette* dated 25 April 1867. It reported that the nobility, gentry, tradesmen and workmen had formed the club together. Unfortunately the first two mentioned parted, in racing terms, with the necessary cash. The very first match was against West Worthing who narrowly won by one run.

One of the golden ages of Findon cricket was in the early 1900s when Brigadier H.G. Wyatt reformed and directed the club. Both the First and Second World Wars interrupted cricket at Findon but then Major Spen Hiller, a fusilier, almost single-handedly turned the ground back from being an Army tank and vehicle store to the present cricket venue. It is an impressive setting with the South Downs in the background and horses grazing in the fields below.

Findon is an attractive village where markets have been held on Nepcote Green since the thirteenth century. It is famous for the Sheep Fair, which has been an annual event since it began in the eighteenth century. There are two old pubs very close to each other – the Gun Inn and the Village House. Both pubs are well known in the horse-racing world as they have been patronised by the local celebrated trainers over the years. Josh Gifford and his son Nick train their racehorses on the South Downs just east of Findon. Both father and son have been very close to the cricket club for many years. As a jockey Josh was a National Hunt winner four times and since then he has trained 1,586 horses, of which 700 were winners. The highlight of Josh's career was when he trained Aldaniti, which won the Grand National in 1981. The winning jockey was Bob Champion, who previously had been struggling against cancer.

FIRLE PLACE

At the start of the eighteenth century the development of cricket had advanced and the game interested some wealthy patrons who financed their own teams. These patrons vied with each other as to who possessed the champion team and this led to the county matches as played today.

Sir William Gage and the 2nd Duke of Richmond were pioneers and promoters of Sussex cricket. The Gage family had been at Firle Place since 1496. In 1725 Sir William received a letter from the Duke challenging him to a cricket match. His courteous reply to the Duke read:

My Lord Duke,
I received this moment your Grace's letter and am extremely happy your Grace intends us ye honour of making one a Tuesday, and will without fail bring a gentleman with me to play against you, one that has played very seldom for these several years. I am in great affliction from being shamefully beaten yesterday, the first match I played this year. However, I will muster up all my courage against Tuesday's engagement. I will trouble your Grace with nothing more than I wish you Success in everything but ye Cricket Match and that I am etc. etc.

Firle   July ye 16th   W. Gage

Sir William was indeed 'shamefully beaten' at Firle and this was the first record of cricket in the village. But William must have turned in his grave when, in 1951, Firle were dismissed for a total of 6 by Selmeston, the rival neighbouring village. What was even more embarrassing was that 4 of the 6 runs were scored by a Selmeston player on loan to Firle.

Even though Firle has a declining village population today, the club manages to run two teams and three junior XIs. Even as long ago as 1830 the *Brighton Gazette* recorded that Firle CC raised two teams on one Saturday. With all those Firle men playing cricket the question must be asked: who was milking Lord Gage's cows or harvesting that afternoon?

The Ram Inn, which stands by the entrance to the ground, has been the natural headquarters since the eighteenth century. With youngsters coming through the junior sides, cricket at Firle is in a very healthy state. Firle Cricket Club is thriving and it is a far cry away from the days of being 'shamefully beaten'.

GOODWOOD

The earliest known game of cricket at Goodwood was in 1702. A receipt for brandy given to the players records this very first match. In 1727 in Goodwood Park, a game was played between the 2nd Duke of Richmond and Mr Brodrick of Peper Harow Park, near Godalming. A set of rules was drawn up one of which stated that: 'If any of the Gamesters shall speak or give their opinion, on any point of the Game they are to be turned out and voided in the match.' These rules are the oldest set of cricket rules in the world. The originals are kept in Goodwood House, with a copy in the club pavilion and at Lord's.

Goodwood has a strong link with Lord's. The 4th Duke was one of the original backers of Thomas Lord when he bought 'the rough piece of land' in St John's Wood and the 5th Duke was president of the MCC. Another attachment with Lord's are the club colours, which are the racing colours of the Dukes of Richmond. They became the colours of the MCC around 1888.

Goodwood cricketers understandably prefer to play at home under the veil of the vast Cedar of Lebanon tree. This magnificent tree was planted as a seed in 1752 and then four years later planted out on the ground. Opposite the tree is the manicured park stretching out in front of Goodwood House, which was built for the 3rd Duke of Richmond in the late eighteenth century. The famous Goodwood Racecourse is within the 12,000 acres of the Goodwood Estate. The Glorious Goodwood meeting was first introduced by the 4th Duke of Richmond in 1814. Today it is one of the major summer events of the sporting calendar.

HEATHFIELD PARK

Heathfield was a tiny community in the thirteenth century and life centred around the parish church of All Saints and the Star Inn. The outside of the church looks much as it did and inside there is an inscription in memory of General George Augustus Eliott, who later became Lord Heathfield in 1787. A remarkable soldier, he raised his own regiment and took part in the siege of Havana in 1762. With his share of the prize money he bought Heathfield Park.

The Star became an inn around 1388. It inn is very popular locally and it also attracts visitors from all over the world. Today the parish church of All Saints is very well supported by the villagers. The annual fête, with all the various stalls and the band playing, is always a highlight of the year. Meanwhile, at Heathfield Park, the cricket club continues to benefit from recent developments such as a new scorebox with electronic scoring system.

The earliest record of cricket being played on the present site dates back to 1878, although cricket was doubtless played within the confines of Heathfield Park prior to this. For many years the ground, in its idyllic setting, was part of the Heathfield Park estate, and the club played there by kind permission of the successive owners on nominal terms.

HENFIELD

The claim that Henfield is one of the oldest clubs in the country is confirmed by the earliest reference to Henfield cricket in the diary of Thomas Marchant of Hurstpierpoint. In the entry of 4 June 1719 he records 'a cricket match in the Sandfields with Henfield'. Later, the Sackville Papers of 1745 refer to Henfield's first named cricketer – 'Martin of Henfield played for Sussex against Surrey at Berry Hill'. There is also evidence of the first cricket played on the common from the *Sussex Weekly*

Advertiser of September 1764: 'On Henfield Common between Arundel Club and the east part of this county'. In 1771 Henfield played Lewes and also had a game against Coulsdon in Surrey – the first time that Henfield played outside the county.

The first scorecard for a match on the common was between the Gentlemen of the Weald and the Gentlemen of Broadwater in June 1793. In July of the same year another scorecard records the first Henfield match on the common where the club has enjoyed longstanding fixtures spanning 200 years.

Henfield village was once an important staging post and it has two old coaching inns. The church is Saxon and dates back to a charter of AD 770. One of the most unusual buildings in the village is a sixteenth-century cottage known as the 'Cat House'. Inside there are stencils on the eaves of cats with their paws outstretched as if chasing birds. A former owner of the cottage believed that the vicar's cat had eaten his canary.

LURGASHALL

Lurgashall has a classic village green. It is triangular with very attractive cottages surrounding this archetypal English country scene. The green is in itself a meeting-point with the little post office (where 'humbugs' and boiled sweets are still kept in large jars) on one side and the Noah's Ark pub opposite. Next door to the pub is the pretty village church. Once again the village triangular syndrome exists – church, pub and cricket green! Lurgashall's name is significant, if the conjectures of the place-name experts are correct, for it comes from the Old English *lytel goers-healh*, which means 'little grazing land'.

Common to most village cricket clubs, Lurgashall teams often included characters from a wide selection of the local community. Gary Sharp, the blacksmith's son, has played cricket for Lurgashall for the last fifty years and he is now the groundsman, and the Lawson family have also been stalwarts of the club for many years. The club continues to hold the very popular six-a-side competition. On this occasion the ball is carted to all corners of the green – even into bordering cottage gardens causing frustrated fielders to search among the flowerbeds. This event raises funds to support, for example, the cricket pavilion, formerly the blacksmith's yard. From this roof-tiled building, with its attractive clock perched on top, it is only a few steps to stroll to the pub – so often a watering hole for the weary players.

Cricket has been played on this same village green for the last 250 years. One article from the *West Sussex Gazette* dated 1858 records a match played

on the village green against the local neighbours and rivals Ebernoe: 'The game stood with Lurgashall needing only another 3 runs to win and with still 7 wickets left. There was enough light to score at least another 30 to 40 runs but the Ebernoe players decided that they had had enough of it and promptly pulled the stumps out of the ground thus ending the game.'

MAYFIELD

The earliest reference to a cricket match involving Mayfield was on Monday 28 May 1750. Another diary recorded a match played at Mayfield against the county (or pretended county) in August 1756. The Mayfield side would have been composed of employees on the Mayfield Manor. As well as iron and forestry workers, there were some wealthy landowners in the team. Also included in these early matches would be players known as 'gamesters' (latter-day professional 'ringers') who would be paid by the patron or organiser. He would recoup the expenses paid out by raising betting wagers on the outcome of the match or individual performances by the players.

The worst result ever suffered by a Mayfield side was in 1861 when Sheffield Park bowled Mayfield out for 8 runs in the first innings and then for only 11 in the second. Mayfield were in sombre mood following this calamitous result. To make matters worse, one of the players had picked up the ball while batting and was given out. At least this experience produced a more positive outlook by the players and prepared the ground for the formation of Mayfield Cricket Club five years later.

In the early 1900s Mayfield staged their cricket week. This would be a grand occasion when the local gentry would entertain guests in the marquees around the ground. Sussex county players would be part of the

festivities and this attracted a vast number of spectators. The 1920s and 1930s were successful years for Mayfield and in the late 1950s the club increased the number of fixtures and against improved opposition. Mayfield Cricket Club has seen social and demographic changes over the years. In the early days the players were nearly all locals who seldom ventured outside the village boundaries. But with the improvement of the roads and the construction of the railway link in 1880, Mayfield became more accessible to visitors. Today the village is as attractive as ever and the cricket club flourishes thanks to the dedication and resolve of many people from different walks of life.

PARHAM PARK

Parham Park, between Storrington and Pulborough, is one of the most beautiful cricket grounds in the country. The game was first played in 1898 when the Lord Zouche gave his permission for 'the young men of Parham to play cricket in the Park'. In the following year the ground was laid out in its present position and a match was played between Parham and local neighbours Storrington. Unfortunately the game turned out to be an inauspicious baptism for hosts Parham as they lost by an innings and 22 runs, skittled out for 14 in the first innings (H. West scored 12 of these runs) and an improved 17 (H. West did not feature) in the second. The club was drawn entirely from workers on the estate right up to the 1950s. Since then the membership has been drawn from local villages and as far afield as Hove and Worthing.

Before the pavilion was built in 1954, the players had to put up a marquee before each game and dismantle it afterwards. Parham used to play both days on the weekend, but now the club just enjoys playing friendly matches on Sundays. To celebrate its centenary, Parham Park CC jetted out to California for a cricket tour. There they played matches against a Hollywood CC in Los Angeles and then a match in San Francisco. The club have the enviable advantage of playing cricket in such an idyllically situated ground in the heart of a medieval deer park, on the slopes of the South Downs.

PARHAM HOUSE

In 1540, at the Dissolution of the Monastery of Westminster, Henry VIII granted the manor of Parham to Robert Palmer, whose family had originated from Sussex. In 1577 his two-year-old grandson laid the foundation stone of the new and larger house and Parham has remained a family home ever since. It was bought by the Pearson family in 1922 and was first opened to visitors in 1948, after the Second World War, during which it had been a home to evacuee children and Canadian soldiers.

Mr and Mrs Pearson spent more than sixty years carefully restoring Parham, filling it with a fine collection of old furniture, paintings and textiles. There is a magnificent four-acre walled garden and within the eighteenth-century pleasure grounds are a lake and many specimen trees. Only a short distance from the manor is a small church, which is probably of sixteenth-century origin. It was largely rebuilt and the tower was added around 1800-1820. The church is all that remains of the old village of Parham.

Parham House and the cricket field are surrounded by some 875 acres of working agricultural and forestry land. Within the estate are 300 acres of ancient deer park, dating back to 1628. It is a marvellous setting for cricket with fallow deer at times roaming around the boundary and both the manor house and the Sussex South Downs in the background.

PETWORTH PARK

Petworth Park Cricket Club began in 1823 when the matches were played between Petworth House and the lake. The club still play on the grounds of the 700-acre park landscaped by Capability Brown in 1752. Tall horse chestnut trees stand between the ground and Petworth House.

Petworth House was built between 1688 and 1696 and it is now in the hands of the National Trust. The cricket ground, situated between the magnificent seventeenth-century mansion and the lake, held the most famous matches ever played by West Sussex. On 3 June 1837, the *West Sussex Gazette* reported on the match at Petworth between West Sussex and East Sussex. Here were the Sussex champions head to head: the two Broadridges, the Lillywhites and Lanaway, the steady underarm bowler. James Lillywhite was only twenty when he first played for Sussex. He was a left-arm medium-pace bowler and very strong with the bat too. Many of the Sussex players wielded home-grown bats from the county.

The early life of a cricket bat began just outside Petworth. The willow trees were grown along the banks of the Rother from Rotherbridge to Petworth Station. It took some ten to fifteen years to produce a tree twenty to thirty feet high with a butt of 24-30in. Usually only the best clean length of butt was taken by the manufacturers of quality bats.

SINGLETON

In 1953 Singleton and West Dean formed a joint team. But everyone longed for cricket to return to the village of Singleton. In 1963 the club obtained use of the present ground Sheepwash Meadow.

The pavilion came from a seventeenth-century Sussex barn near Haywards Heath. Each beam was numbered for reassembly and the barn was taken apart and transported to Singleton. It took three years to put together and was finally opened in 1981. Singleton Cricket Club has been enjoying matches for over 250 years. It was in 1747, the year Admiral Hawke defeated the French fleet, that the first recorded ladies' match was played on a major ground. On 13 July that year, the 'Maids' of Singleton and Charlton played those of West Dean and Chilgrove. The match took place on the Artillery Ground at Finsbury, the forerunner of Lord's. Total gate receipts were over £80 (a vast amount of money at the time) and there were reported to be 3,200 spectators at this well-advertised and greatly anticipated match. The game itself was dramatic as 'rowdies' broke into the ground and began fighting. The organiser defused the dangerous maul by wielding a whip to protect the players. Eventually play was suspended until the following morning.

Singleton is famous for the Weald & Downland Open Air Museum which opened in 1971. There are over forty reconstructed historical rural buildings from all over south-east England. Constructions on view include a Wealden farmhouse, a charcoal-burning hut, a working blacksmith's forge and a watermill from Lurgashall. The museum is situated in an impressive 50-acre park close to the village.

SLINDON

Slindon is one of the oldest surviving cricket clubs in England. In 1740 Slindon had become so famous that they beat an All-England XI made up from the best players in the rest of Sussex, Surrey, Kent and Hampshire. After the match at Merrow Down, near Guildford, Slindon's patron, the 2nd Duke of Richmond, wrote from his seat at Goodwood House to the Duke of Newcastle at his residence in Surrey: 'Poore little Slyndon beat your whole county in almost one innings'.

One of the greatest cricket matches ever played was on Monday 18 June 1742 in the Artillery Ground, London when the County of Kent played against All England. Kent won the match but in the All England side were no less than four players from Slindon. That same season Slindon played forty-three matches and lost only one. Slindon then played against 'The eleven picked gentlemen of London', again at the Artillery Ground: 'There will be the greatest number of people that ever was known on a like occasion, it is hoped, nay desired, that gentlemen will not crowd in by reason of a very large sum of money is laid that one of the Sussex gentleman gets 40 notches himself.' In those day the runs were recorded by the scorer making notches in either a hazel or ash stick called a 'notching stick'.

The 'Sussex gentleman' could only be the great batsman from Slindon, Richard Newland. In this match Newland scored less than 40 runs but in the 1745 England v. Kent game he scored 88. Not only did he lead Slindon for many years, he also captained England. His nephew, Richard Nyren, learned cricket from his famous uncle and later became captain of the famous Hambledon club. Richard Newland is buried near the main entrance of Slindon's twelfth-century flint-built village church.

Slindon was the estate village for Slindon House. Today the Slindon Estate is owned by the National Trust and most of the village comes under its care. Slindon House was originally founded as a residence for the Archbishop of Canterbury. The house is now a school called Slindon College.

TILLINGTON

The earliest-known mention of the club is in 1785 when Tillington played games at Reading, Portsmouth and Farnham. Villagers from Northchapel and Petworth helped to make up the team. In 1822 the club was aligned with villagers once again, this time from Duncton, and from 1826 only neighbouring Petworth remained a 'partner village' with Tillington. The club, now playing in its own right, was certainly in existence in 1906 when the matches were played at Pitshill, not far from the present ground. Cricket matches at this current ground at Upperton began around 1934. The ground, overlooking the valley from Petworth to the South Downs is one of the most attractive in Sussex. It is always a popular venue for visiting teams who enjoy not only the cricket but also the breathtaking views and the homemade teas.

Tillington village dates back to the days before the Norman Conquest and it appeared in the Domesday Book as 'Tolinstone'. The village lies beside the western walls of Petworth House. All Hallow's church also stands adjacent to these walls and it is a local landmark with the tower topped by stone pinnacles. Both Turner and Constable have painted the church and its tower.

The Horse Guards Inn is the other noticeable landmark. It was originally called the New Star but was renamed in 1840 in honour of the Horse Guards, who enjoyed a welcome rest and drink in between transporting gold from London to Portsmouth, or even hunting local smugglers and highwaymen.

WISBOROUGH GREEN

Wisborough Cricket Club was founded around 1876. In the early days the opponents were from the local area – places like Billingshurst, Petworth, Horsham and Loxwood. In the 1950s, 1960s and 1970s the fixture card was widened and Wisborough became one of the most respected cricket clubs in Sussex. Over the years, Wisborough Cricket Club has played host to many charity teams such as the Lord's Taverners. Comedians Harry Secombe, Leslie Crowther, Jimmy Edwards and Bernard Cribbins have all played on the green in helping to raise funds for national charities. More recently Phil Collins, Phil Tuffnell, John Emburey and Derek Pringle have all played for the Wilting Willows team.

Surrounding the pretty rectangular green are half-timbered tile-hung cottages and elegant horse chestnut trees. There are also weatherboarding and

brick houses dotted about this generous cricket green. Nearby, the village church of St Peter ad Vincula dates back to Norman times and the walls of the church are almost five feet thick, with a door some thirteen feet high. It was thought that the door was on the site of an Anglo-Saxon keep and the reason for its enormous height was to enable a horseman to pass through.

Wisborough was one of the main villages in the Weald and even today it still has two areas of preserved woodland. In the sixteenth and seventeenth centuries, the village was an important industrial centre, particularly as it had inexhaustible amounts of trees for building houses and ships and also for the iron industry.

SURREY

ABINGER HAMMER

The cricket ground lies alongside the fast-flowing stream. Players fielding deep on the boundary have to be very aware of the water hazard immediately behind them.

Village cricket has been played at Abinger since 1870. The club moved to the present ground at Hammer Marsh in 1930 – a memorial to the Abinger men who fell in the First World War. Over the past few years the club has gone through a great deal of development and now the Abinger Sports Club not only enjoys cricket and tennis but lively social events incorporating both a big band and a jazz band.

An important local industry was iron and this is reflected in the village's name, Abinger Hammer. The hammers were water-driven in the village forges. The 'Hammer' takes its name not from the hammer clock ('Jack the Smith') but from an old forge where cannonballs were made in the sixteenth century. The distinctive clock, erected in 1909, overhangs the main road. Abinger enjoys celebrity cricket matches in association with Surrey County Beneficiary and this provides the necessary finance to make Abinger such a thriving club today.

BROOK

The club was formed in 1923 with the title of 'The Brook and Sandhills Cricket Club' (Sandhills being the hamlet adjacent to Brook). In the early days and up to and including the Second World War, keenly contested matches were played against local village sides. Following these games, the players only had to cross the road for the evening's entertainment in the handily placed Dog & Pheasant. Today the routine on match days is very much the same. After the war horizons expanded, with the fixture list including clubs from further afield, from the south coast to London. These new fixtures attracted quality players but still the matches tended to be 'friendlies'. However, in the late 1980s the pressure for league cricket was irresistible if the club was going to continue attracting good players (and their supporters).

The ground, surrounded by mature trees, is one of the prettiest in Surrey and cricketers relish the chance to play at Brook.

CHIDDINGFOLD

hiddingfold is a quintessential English village. It has a thirteenth-century church with a peal of eight bells, one of which is believed to be around 500 years old. The village green has many handsome cottages and the Crown Inn is a most impressive hostelry, claimed to be the oldest in England. There are records to show that the inn was first mentioned in 1383. Edward VI is reported to have stayed at the Crown Inn in the fifteenth century.

The outbreak of the Second World War restricted cricket activities and the original ground on Mill Lane was ploughed up to grow potatoes. Cricket is now played at the Woodside Lane Ground where Chiddingfold celebrated their 200th anniversary in 2004. Like many Wealden cricket clubs, Chiddingfold started playing league cricket in the mid-1990s. The friendly fixtures on Sundays still make cricket a prominent part of Chiddingfold village life.

COLDHARBOUR

Coldharbour cricket ground is the highest ground in the south of England and it must be one of the highest in the UK. It lies above the village of Coldharbour, 800 feet above sea level on Leith Hill. The ground, with its almost square shape and wonderful setting, was moved to the present position in 1950. It became impossible to play cricket on the village ground because a road cut right through Coldharbour.

The pavilion is quite unique: It was transported by lorry from Kenley Aerodrome where it had been used for stores. There are no services so water has to be brought up in containers for each game. There is certainly not enough water for showers or to water the wicket. Trees had to be cut down and holes filled in the ground. The boundary was marked by angle posts and wire left over from the defences on the hill during the war. In spite of the troubles to maintain the ground and the pitch, the renowned head groundsman from The Oval, Harry Brind, visited Coldharbour with a television crew to film how they put the ground to bed at the end of a season as compared to the famous Oval ground. He praised the Coldharbour groundsman for the excellent wickets and the state of the ground in spite of the lack of water.

From the remarkable 'table-top' location with breathtaking views over the Surrey countryside, the small ground is surrounded by a post-and-rail fence and chicken wire to prevent the rabbits doing too much damage. Like many unique cricket grounds there are local cricket laws. To score a six the ball has to clear this surrounding fence, otherwise it is a four. Spare boxes of cricket balls are always essential items to bring up to the ground on match days! Coldharbour's finest moment was in 1991 when the club and the entire village decamped to The Oval for a special celebration match to mark Reg Comber's fiftieth anniversary of playing for the club.

Coldharbour provides village cricket at its very best in this outstanding location. After the game players return to the village 200 feet below, where they can enjoy the landlord's own brewed beer at the Plough Inn.

FOREST GREEN

Cricket was first played in the village of Forest Green in 1895. Initially the home ground was in an estate called Pratsham Grange, which was close to the village. Then, in the early 1900s, the ground moved to its present location on the green. In those days there were enough residents from the village to form two sides on a Saturday, although changing facilities were somewhat alfresco. A tent was erected before each game in the top corner of the ground and if a player needed to 'spend a penny' it was a regular case of third tree from the left. The playing area of the ground was fenced off to protect it from the villagers' grazing animals. The present pavilion had to be transported from its original site at North Holmwood with the help of a cart and some loyal Forest Green stalwarts.

In the early 1950s Ken Cuthbert moved to the village and he captained the team for many years. Those fortunate enough to have played with or against him will have many a story to tell. He was keen to see the club progress and in 1962 he instigated the introduction of a bar, making Forest Green one of the first village cricket clubs in the area to provide such a facility. With the introduction of Sunday matches, Ken placed an advertisement in *The Times* in an attempt to encourage more players:

> WANTED: 'DRINKING CRICKETERS AND CRICKET CLUBS TO PLAY ON SATURDAYS AND SUNDAYS IN A PICTURESQUE SURREY VILLAGE.'

This aroused the interest of the media. Ken was summoned to the television studios and asked to explain the advertisement. The exposure of Forest Green Cricket Club to millions of TV viewers resulted in many new cricketers (not just drinking ones) coming to play and plenty of offers by cricket clubs for new fixtures. Now cricket continues to be played in the tranquil setting at the foot of Leith Hill and just a short stroll up and over the green to many a highwayman's hiding place at the Parrot Inn.

FRENSHAM

The Hallowdene ground at Frensham Cricket Club is set among heathland with farmland dotted around it. It is the ideal location for taking the family out to watch the cricket and enjoy a picnic.

On 13 July 1899 at a dinner in the Mariner's Inn, Frensham, the Reverend W.H. Moody expressed a wish that 'Frensham should get a name for the good conduct of the rising lads of the place. A level piece of ground is ready to play a match this afternoon.' Applause came from all the assembled, and so it was that over 100 years ago the Frensham Cricket Club took the field.

In 1939 Frensham moved from their Pierrepont premises to the Hallowdene ground where they play today. As with most clubs, the war years were a difficult period for cricket at Frensham, but in 1949 extensive work was done on the ground. The development continued through the 1950s, with many of the members helping out. It was their hard labours and endeavour that now allows provision for cricket at Hallowdene today. Nearby are Frensham's Great and Little Ponds. These two sizeable National Trust-owned lakes provide good bird-watching and recreational facilities contained within a 1,000-acre country park.

HAMBLEDON

In 1937, Hambledon, Surrey, played their first match against Hambledon, Hampshire on the historic ground of Broadhalfpenny on Windmill Down. It turned out to be an extremely exciting game with the hosts scoring 166. In reply the Surrey Hambledon batsman hit a six off the last ball to win the match.

Mary Parker has lived most of her life in Hambledon, a pretty village five miles south of Godalming. In her book *Memories of Hambledon* she writes about the early days of the village cricket green: 'The grass was nibbled down by geese, and I was amused one day to see an old lady lunging with her umbrella at an oncoming goose, which promptly bit the end off.' The first Hambledon cricket teams were all local men. During the tea break there were often as many as 200 present (including 'comparative strangers' who had stopped by while motoring past the attractive setting). After the match cider and beer barrels were transported to the pavilion. Over the years the ground has been extended and in May 2004 the new pavilion was completed. Hambledon is now one of the most pleasant village grounds in the country.

Hambledon was originally an old scattered settlement and in the village there are some exceptionally eye-catching buildings. The church is fourteenth century in parts and there are some good sixteenth and seventeenth-century cottages – such as the School Cottage, Malthouse Cottage and Malthouse Farm. Just up a winding land is Court Farm, with its tile-hung roof, and the old granary both positioned next door to the church. Very close to the cricket green is Oakhurst Cottage, a small sixteenth-century twin-framed dwelling owned by the National Trust. It has been restored and furnished as a simple labourer's cottage.

HOLMBURY ST MARY

This attractive ground has been the home of Holmbury St Mary Cricket Club since 1894. Holmbury Hill is 857 feet above sea level and it is one of the highest grounds in the south of England. Originally a flattish plateau covered with grass, gorse, heather and bracken, it was offered to the club on its formation in 1892 but not until two years and many working parties later was it deemed fit for play.

In 1923 the owner Sir Richard Bray, in an attempt to preserve the private nature of the ground, enclosed the outfield with solid wooden posts and wire. The original posts can be seen in the picture below.

The only way to arrive at this lovely wooded ground is by a very hilly undulating track and before this was laid, at the end of the Second World War, all the players and tea ladies had to trek wearily up the path with their cricket kit bags and the necessary tea accessories. Water was only laid on in the 1950s and electricity wasn't available until 1979.

Until 1879 the village was called Felday and it was notorious for smugglers and sheep-stealers. Then, in the Victorian era, Holmbury St Mary became a village for 'well-to-do' people. Holmbury Hill has Leith Hill as its taller neighbour. Hidden in the undergrowth of the hillside are the remains of an eight-acre Iron Age hill fort.

OCKLEY

Tucked under the well-wooded background of Leith Hill is one of the largest and prettiest 'classic' village greens (600 feet wide at one point). The pleasure of Ockley is in its setting, its atmosphere and its pubs, the Cricketers and the Red Lion, which are both seventeenth century. It was at the Red Lion Inn that the very first meeting was held on 25 June 1852 when 'it was resolved that the following Rules and Regulations be adopted for the Management of the Club:

Rule V: That if any Member be intoxicated or make use of indecent language or swear during a match, and shall not desist from it, he shall forfeit the sum of one shilling. Any player smoking when engaged in the field will also be fined one shilling.

Rule VI: That on Tuesdays and Fridays there will be practices at precisely half-past six. Any player having got five runs will be asked to lay down his bat (retire) and if any player be at the wickets for an unreasonably long time without taking a run, he will also be asked to lay down his bat.'

Ockley is steeped in history: the village once stood on Stane Street, the old Roman road between Chichester and London. The road was known as Brandy or Silk Street due to the fact that it a was smuggling route. In the mid-ninth century, reputedly near to the village, King Ethelwulf of the West Saxons had a fierce battle against the marauding Vikings. After the Norman invasion, the woodlands surrounding Ockley were defined as a royal hunting forest. Sadly nothing remains of the Norman fortification close to the village green, but the fourteenth-century church of St Margaret has survived and was rebuilt in 1873.

Ockley's location makes it a perfect scene for either playing or watching cricket – and even a visit to the Red Lion Inn where the cricket club first began.

OUTWOOD

The first known reference to cricket at the club was in 1835, a time when the famous cricketer William Lambert (1779-1851) lived in the village. He first appeared for Surrey against England in 1801, and he was the first player to score a century in both innings at Lord's in 1817. Unfortunately he made an untimely exit from the game for allegedly 'selling' a match.

This very attractive ground was bequeathed to the National Trust in 1955. Since then, Outwood has hosted many famous matches involving both county and international players. In 1979 Outwood played Argentina as part of their essential preparations for the then Prudential World Cup.

The current pavilion was built at a cost of £198 in 1897, the year of Queen Victoria's Golden Jubilee. Close to the cricket ground, the Outwood Post Mill is generally acknowledged to be the oldest working windmill in England.

PEPER HAROW

Peper Harow has a special place in the history of cricket. On 21 August 1727 a match was played between the 2nd Duke of Richmond's team from Goodwood and Mr A. Brodrick's side from 'Pepperharowe' (as it was known then). The importance of this match in the development of cricket was that a set of rules were drawn up by the Duke and Mr Brodrick. Copies of these rules are kept at both Goodwood House and Lord's.

To celebrate the 250th anniversary of this historical match, The Gentlemen of Pepperharowe met the Duke of Richmond's XII in a charity game on the Peper Harow estate in July 1977. The players kept to the original set of rules. The underarm bowlers had just four deliveries in their over and the fielders could only return the ball underarm and not throw it back. There was no leg-before or stumping and only the wicketkeeper or bowler could run a batsman out. Two scorers sat well inside the field of play carving their notches as each run was scored on their 'notching stick'. In this anniversary match well-known personalities from the theatre and television took part – all wearing the dress of the time with breeches and stockings and umpires in full-skirted coats and three-cornered hats. The Duke of Richmond's XII were eventually victors by 18 runs with Godfrey Evans, the great England wicketkeeper (sporting luxuriant side-whiskers), running out the last Peper Harow player.

Records of Peper Harow go back to Saxon times. In the Domesday Book of 1086 there is mention of the estate of 'Pipereherge' covering 300 acres. The church of St Nicholas was built in Norman times and the ancient yew tree in the churchyard is believed to be over 600 years old. Peper Harow House was built in 1768 and the park surrounding the house was designed by Capability Brown in 1763.

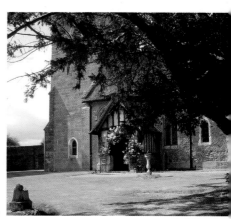

SHACKLEFORD

Shackleford is a relative newcomer compared to many village cricket clubs. It was after the Second World War, when the Canadian army occupied Shackleford Heath, that the firm Hewitts used the field for their employees to play sport. In 1951 a proper square was laid and matches were played on both Saturdays and Sundays. The teams were of quite a high standard and there was always a good 'local derby' game against nearby Puttenham village. By the 1970s there wasn't a Hewitts employee in sight on the cricket field and in 1979 the cricket club was officially formed. There were still some competitive matches but the ethos of the club had moved towards more social friendly games. In 1984 the committee decided that a 'new' pavilion was needed. The club members and locals were all very excited. But it was not the sort of pavilion most cricketers would dream of – it was an old school classroom. Sections arrived piece by piece and a loan was taken out for the cost of erecting the pavilion. During the 1990s the Shackleford teams mainly consisted of members living or working in the village. Very often the captain could call upon the services of players just down the road at Aldro School. The club link with the school still remains.

Shackleford's brief history is a fairly typical story of many little village clubs. Most of these struggle for money and fewer clubs have 'real' villagers in the team. What has become evident in village cricket in the twenty-first century is that very few clubs exist on playing purely friendlies. Most village clubs are forced to join leagues to attract players from outside and also to attract local sponsors.

Shackleford had grown into a small village by the middle of the eighteenth century. Nowadays it is one of the prettiest in Surrey. Originally the cricket ground was simply a cow field. A batsman really could hit the ball into 'cow corner'. Conveniently for the cricketers, the Cyder House Inn stands just yards down the lane. Shackleford cricket, with its friendly approach, will continue to be enjoyed for many seasons ahead.

TILFORD

Tilford's cricketing fame reflects two main influences: the association with 'Silver' Billy Beldham and its classical setting. Beldham (1766-1862) was a titan of the Georgian game, from which he retired in 1822 to become landlord of the Barley Mow. This ancient pub and the Tilford Green is claimed to be the setting for A.G. Macdonell's classic novel *England, Their England*.

The Barley Mow (which Beldham's ghost is said to frequent), a church, two ancient bridges and overhanging oaks continue to provide the ideal backdrop for village cricket. The 17ft drop from one side of the ground to the other and a boundary encompassing three roads can challenge the fielders. Despite these imperfections, the green continues to entice advertisers looking for a quintessential old English village cricket scene.

Tilford Green is reputedly one of the oldest grounds in England. Although the present club dates from 1885, there is evidence of cricket being played at the village much earlier.

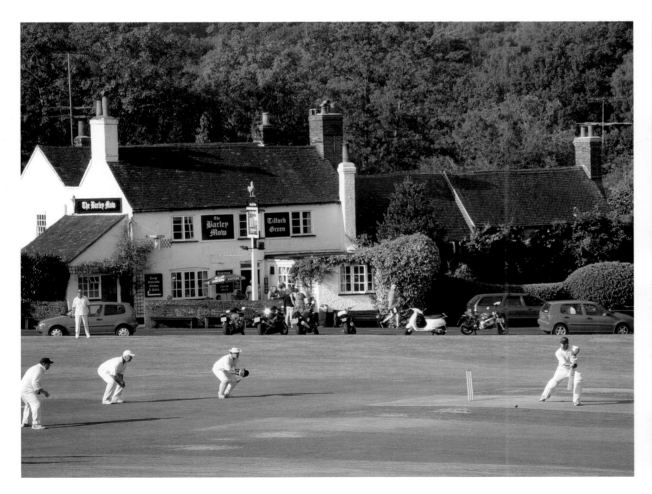

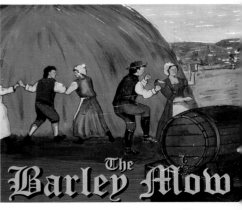

HAMPSHIRE

HAMBLEDON

Hambledon is often referred to as 'The Cradle of Cricket'. It is the village whose cricket first became widely recognised as the heart of the English game. The club was founded around 1750 and the game first played on the Broadhalfpenny ground. The Reverend Charles Powlett spent thirty years assembling the very best players from neighbouring counties – the 'Hambledon Heroes'. Richard Newland moved from Slindon, Sussex to Hambledon in 1755. His nephew Richard Nyren was the landlord of the famous Bat & Ball Inn across the road from the ground. Richard captained the team in its great days and his son John, like his father a fine player, wrote about those glorious times in the 'Cradle of Cricket.' Among the players, John Small was an outstanding cricketer as well as a cricket bat and ball maker. Thomas Brett was one of the fastest bowlers in the game. The 'keeper of the wicket' was Tom Seuter, who often stood up when keeping to Brett. No pads in those days either! 'Lumpy' Stevens was the demon underarm spinner. He was true to his nickname when once, at the Bat & Ball after a match, he was seen to eat a whole apple pie.

There were many memorable matches at Hambledon and the Bat & Ball ground would be packed with crowds often a thousand strong. Many players and spectators alike would ride to the ground by horse or by carriage. There was great excitement and plenty of vocal support and advice to the batsmen: 'Go hard! Go Hard! Tich and turn! Tich and turn!' In those days the batsmen had to touch the umpire's stick before turning round and setting off for a second run.

By the 1770s cricket had reached a new level and consistency of performance. The Hambledon players had led the way. Brawn had been replaced by beauty. This was a time of inventiveness in both batting and bowling. With the introduction of the third stump the batsman now adopted the straight bat method. The bowling was much more pitched up in the style of the 'length' delivery. The modern game was born.

HURSTBOURNE PRIORS

The village of Hurstbourne Priors rests in the north-west corner of Hampshire. The writer William Cobbett makes reference to the village and calls it 'Downhusband' in his book *Rural Rides*. The cricket ground is set against the backdrop of the parish church nestled among lofty trees. This scene was painted by the renowned cricket artist Jocelyn Galsworthy.

Cricket has been played in Hurstbourne Priors for around 100 years. The village residents constructed the existing timber-clad and thatched pavilion in the early 1930s using materials supplied by the owner at that time, Lord Portsmouth. The freehold for the ground was subsequently conveyed to Hurstbourne Priors Parish Council in 1953. Records, however, go back to the 1800s when the club, then known as Hurstbourne Park CC, hosted the MCC. The scorebook from this fixture is still held by the club.

The club became involved in league cricket in the late 1980s and now they play in the regional zone of the Hampshire Cricket League. By its very nature the cricket has become more competitive but the focus remains firmly on the social side of the game. Recent improvements have been made to the pavilion and today Hurstbourne Priors is one of the best cricket venues in the south of England.

LONGPARISH

'The position of Ground Man was offered to J. Hayter at a gratuity of £1 & 1 shilling.' This minute comes from a report of a meeting held in Longparish in 1886. Although cricket had been played before, this meeting saw the official formation of Longparish Cricket Club.

In those days Mr Hayter would have used a hand mower to cut a narrow strip of grass in someone's field and then he would roll it with a horse-drawn roller. The very early matches were all friendlies but there was a healthy amount of rivalry between the nearby villages. In 1903 the annual dinner at the Plough cost two shillings and two years later the club invested in a new heavy roller costing £17. The then treasurer had to dip into his pockets and find the extra £3 8s 1d to balance the books. The club moved to their new ground in the middle of the village in 1913. Few details remain of the matches between the wars as many reports perished in a fire at the home of one of the club officials. He was known to be a reckless individual who, while driving with a loaded twelve-bore shotgun in his car, inadvertently blew a hole through the roof.

Longparish is not only renowned for its cricket prowess but also for its teas. The 'Tea Ladies' first became an organised team of very important helpers in the 1930s. Originally the tea water was boiled in a wood-burning copper at the back of the pavilion. Collecting sticks and keeping the fire going was the job of the 'copper boy', who was bribed with a free tea – but only if the fire didn't go out.

In 1972 Longparish entered both the new Hampshire Cricket League and also the National Village Knock-Out Cup. The club attracted some very adept players in the 1970s and it was no surprise that they became league champions in 1979. The following year even more success arrived when not only were the team league champions again but the highlight of the season was to reach the final of the National Village Cup at Lord's. The semi-final against Troon was the most exciting match ever played at Longparish. The crowd, numbering over 1,500, was packed around the boundary. There was much excitement, with supporters running onto the field when Longparish finally won with just one over to spare. Most of the village travelled to Lord's for the 'big day out' at the National Village Cup final. It was a marvellous occasion but sadly Longparish were the eventual runners-up. In 1987 there was another near empty village and journey up to Lord's for the Village Cup final. This time Longparish were the victors, beating Treeton Welfare, the Yorkshire champions.

For many years the well-known cricket correspondent of *The Times*, John Woodcock, would organise a team to play at Longparish. His team would be full of star players such as Sir Len Hutton, Richie Benaud and Denis Compton. One year Frank 'Typhoon' Tyson played and was about to bowl. He politely asked the umpire if he could 'bounce' one. The ball was still rising as it cleared the 'keeper's head and landed on the wheel of the sight screen. The umpire resisted the opportunity of signalling 6 byes.

Longparish Cricket continues to thrive and there is every chance of a third visit to Lord's.

OAKLEY

Oakley Cricket Club has a long history and perhaps it is inevitable that there should be some doubt as to the exact year it was officially founded. Research has shown that, although occasional matches were played as early as 1835, the first match took place at the current Oakley Park ground was in 1854. The club was recognized as one of the leading village cricket teams in the county and the *Hampshire Chronicle* of 5 July 1856 reported that 'the cricket ground is now considered the best in Hampshire, if not in England'.

Oakley moved happily into the twentieth century and in 1923 there was a match between Mr Tom Garratt's XI and the Oakley Ladies watched by a crowd of 200. The Ladies were the eventual winners, mainly due to the fact that 'the Gentlemen had to wield broomsticks with their left hands'.

The lovely cricket ground was still in good order but in 1928 there was an invasion of moles. At the AGM it was 'humorously suggested that there was not a mole to be found in any other part of England, as it seemed that the whole family of that species had congregated in Oakley Cricket Park'. At least the groundsman resisted the temptations of copying the actions of the Longparish Cricket Club groundsman who waited patiently at dawn for the moles to surface and then took aim and fired several rounds of his twelve-bore shotgun.

At Oakley there is never a dull moment when fielding since there are either horse-riders going by or the drone of the diesel train just close to the grounds on the London to Southampton line. An old match report recorded that 'as the steam trains rush past, the passengers cluster to the windows, and the monotony of travelling is relieved by a glimpse of the cricketers in their flannel uniform.' Only a short distance from Oakley is Watership Down, high up on a ridge and the setting for the book by Richard Adams.

THE LAST FEW OVERS

Looking back I was so fortunate to discover the unique cricket setting at the Lynton & Lynmouth ground in the Valley of the Rocks, Devon, which gave me the idea of putting this book together. The last two summers have been great fun travelling with friends and exploring the little villages in the Weald countryside such as the historic ground with the windmill at Meopham in Kent. What really made the experience such fun was meeting so many helpful and hospitable cricket people. Each one of the cricket clubs has been good enough to submit some history of their club and often a centenary brochure, which has been so helpful in compiling the book.

There were one or two observations I made during the course of this project. It became apparent that there is a clear difference in ethos throughout the Wealden village cricket clubs. Firstly, there is the village club that purely plays 'friendlies', most likely on a Sunday with the family having a picnic on the boundary. In this book Shackleford and Hambledon in Surrey are perfect examples of this type of club. Secondly, there is the club that began just playing friendly games but found that, in order to enlarge and improve their playing membership and fixture card, necessitated joining a local league. Then finally, there is the club that has been totally involved in league cricket for years and has a wide playing membership, often turning out two teams on a Saturday and a Sunday XI too.

My other observation was how encouraging it was to visit the village clubs that provided cricket for the young and enthusiastic – the colts section. It was so good to see the dads getting involved too and if more clubs can find time for youth cricket, then the future of the game is very bright indeed.

BIBLIOGRAPHY

The History of Cricket: From The Weald to The World, Peter Wynne-Thomas, The Stationery Office, 1997
A History of Cricket, H.S. Altham, George Allen & Unwin, 1926
Start of Play, David Underdown, Allen Lane, The Penguin Press, 2000
A View From Long Off, Paul J. McColl, Consortium Publishing, 2000
Along The South Downs, David Harrison, Cassell London, 1958
Guide To Rural England, Hugh Taylor & Moira McCrossan, Travel Publishing, 2002
The English Village Green, Brian Bailey, Robert Hale, London, 1985
The Shell Book of English Villages, ed. John Hadfield, Peerage Books, 1980
The Barclays World of Cricket, ed. E. W. Swanton, Collins, 1980

PICTURE ACKNOWLEDGEMENTS

'Lumpy' Stevens, Richard Nyren, Tossing For Innings, Alfred Mynn and William Beldham: Courtesy of Marylebone Cricket Club and the Bridgeman Art Library
Broadhalfpenny Ground, Hambledon: Courtesy of John Shakeshaft
All other images belong to the author, Robin Whitcomb

If you are interested in purchasing other books published by Tempus, or in case you have difficulty finding any Tempus books in your local bookshop, you can also place orders directly through our website
www.tempus-publishing.com